HOW BIG IS THE UNIVERSE?

Astronomy Book for 6 Year Olds
Children's Astronomy Books

BABY PROFESSOR
EDUCATION KIDS

Speedy Publishing LLC
40 E. Main St. #1156
Newark, DE 19711
www.speedypublishing.com

In this book, we're going to talk about the size of the universe. So, let's get right to it!

WHAT IS THE UNIVERSE?

The universe is everything. It's all matter and all energy. It's all living things and all nonliving things. It includes light, space, and time as we know it. Before the universe came into existence, scientists believe that there was no matter, no energy, no space, and no time.

HISTORY OF BELIEFS ABOUT THE UNIVERSE

Most early ideas about the universe had the Earth at its center. Some of the Ancient Greeks thought that the universe might go on forever and that it had always existed.

They pictured it as a group of spheres that held the stars, planets, and the Sun. In their pictures, these spheres always circled around the Earth, which was also shown as a sphere.

As astronomers observed more and had a better concept of how gravity worked, a model with the Sun at its center was talked about. In 1543, the Polish astronomer Nicolaus Copernicus thought that the Sun was at the center and that the planets revolved around it. He published a book about his observations. This theory that the Sun was at the center was fought by the Catholic Church.

NICOLAUS COPERNICUS

GIORDANO BRUNO

In 1584, Giordano Bruno, an Italian friar stated that he thought the stars in the sky were the same as our Sun. He was the first person who understood that the Sun was a star. He also believed that the universe was infinite. He was killed by the Church for his beliefs.

Galileo Galilei was an Italian astronomer. He was the first to publish information about what he saw through a telescope. He was also the first to observe the moons of Jupiter. He believed in the Copernican model of the "universe." In 1633, the Church put him under house arrest for his beliefs.

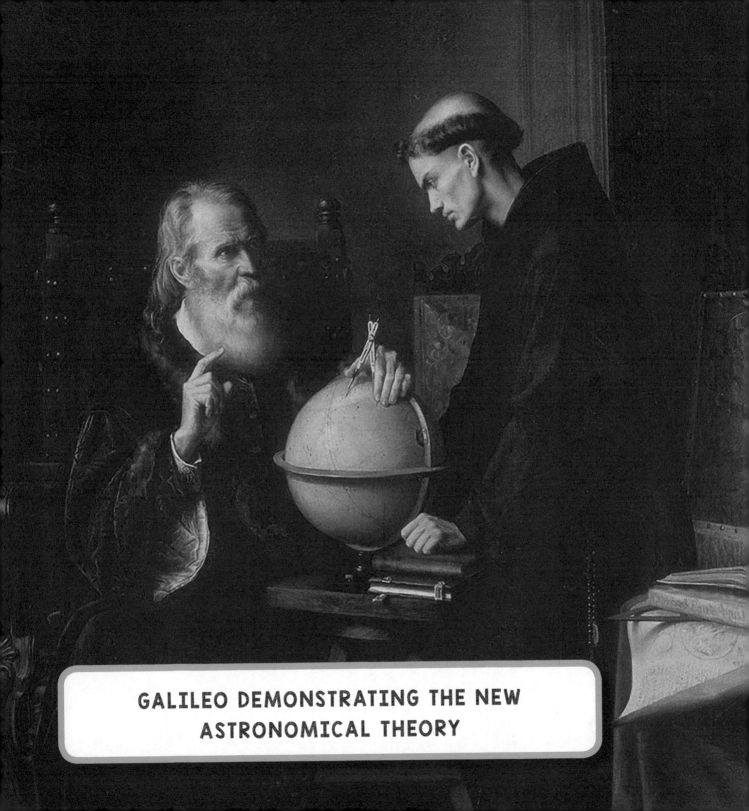

GALILEO DEMONSTRATING THE NEW
ASTRONOMICAL THEORY

GALILEO USING A TELESCOPE

The telescope was invented in the Netherlands in 1608. Galileo used a telescope and he built his own as well. As telescopes continued to improve, it was soon discovered that our Solar System was inside a galaxy, now called the Milky Way. The discovery of spectral lines and redshift led to the understanding of the vast distances in and rapid expansion of the universe.

HOW BIG IS THE UNIVERSE?

The truth is that we don't know everything about the universe. For example, we don't know how big it is. It could be infinite, which essentially means it has no end and goes on forever.

Scientists do have a measurement for what they call the observable universe, which simply means the universe we can see with the telescopes that we have today. They measure the universe in light years. Light travels faster than anything else in the universe.

The distance that light travels in one year is called a light year. Light travels about 186,000 miles in just one second. In an Earth year, the distance that light would travel would be 5.88 trillion miles.

The universe we can see, the observable universe, is all the matter that we can see from Earth today. Light as well as other signals from these distant bodies can be detected from our planet. The diameter of this observable light is 93 billion light years.

If you are looking at a star that's 50 light years away from Earth, then you are seeing how the star looked 50 years ago, not the way it looks today. This is because it took 50 years for the light to travel to the Earth.

THE UNIVERSE IS EXPANDING

One of the problems with measuring the size of the universe is that it's expanding. It's getting larger all the time. In fact, scientists believe the outermost edge is expanding so fast that it's moving more quickly than light travels.

WHAT IS THE UNIVERSE MADE OF?

Our bodies seem tiny when we compare ourselves to the size of the Earth. The Earth seems tiny when you compare it to the size of the Sun. The Sun's mass is over 300,000 times as big as Earth's mass.

The Sun is just one average-sized star in our galaxy. Our galaxy, called the Milky Way, may be made up of as many as 300 billion stars. Each galaxy seems tiny too compared to the universe. Scientists estimate that there are more than 170 billion galaxies in the observable universe.

What's even more amazing is that all these galaxies, planets, and stars we see only take up 5% of the universe. The rest of the universe, 95% of it, is filled up with two things we don't know much about yet. One of them is called dark matter. The other one is called dark energy.

WHAT ARE DARK MATTER AND DARK ENERGY?

Scientists don't yet know what dark matter is. It's a type of matter that isn't ordinary matter. It doesn't give off any electromagnetic radiation. Also, it doesn't interact with light so we can't see it.

Even though scientists can't see dark matter, they are sure it exists because they believe that it's part of the gravitational force that holds galaxies together. Galaxies rotate so fast that they couldn't stay together without this unseen force. Dark matter takes up about 27% of the known universe.

ANDROMEDA GALAXY

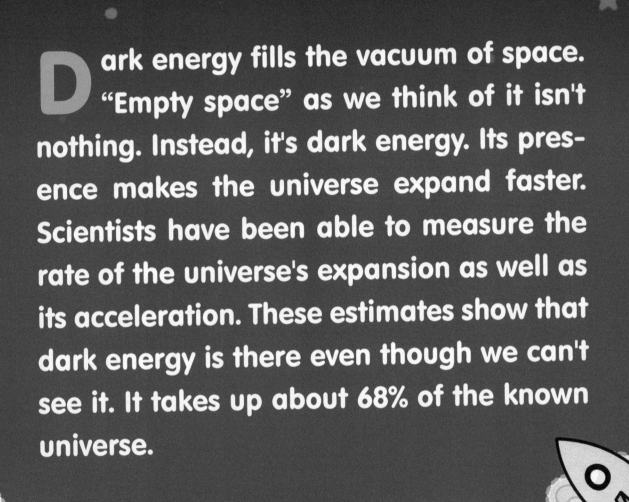

Dark energy fills the vacuum of space. "Empty space" as we think of it isn't nothing. Instead, it's dark energy. Its presence makes the universe expand faster. Scientists have been able to measure the rate of the universe's expansion as well as its acceleration. These estimates show that dark energy is there even though we can't see it. It takes up about 68% of the known universe.

In summary, the universe is made up of:

★ 5% ordinary matter that we can see or detect, such as planets, stars, comets, asteroids, galaxies, dust clouds, etc.

★ 27% dark matter, which we can't see

★ 68% dark energy, which we can't see

HOW OLD IS THE UNIVERSE?

Scientists can tell how long it took the galaxies in the universe to get into their current positions. They can tell how old the universe is by calculating:

★ The current speed of the galaxies

★ The distances to the galaxies from Earth

* The distances of the galaxies from each other

* The rate at which the universe is expanding

* The ages of the oldest star clusters

Astronomers believe that our universe is about 13.8 billion years old.

BIG BANG

WHAT WAS THE BIG BANG?

Astronomers believe that the universe started around 13.8 billion years ago. It was formed from a huge explosion that they call the Big Bang. At this time, we don't know what caused the Big Bang to happen or why it happened. Within the first few seconds, the universe expanded from a size much smaller than an atom to the size of an entire city.

The baby universe starts forming matter. At the beginning, the matter exists as particles and also as antiparticles. Particles and antiparticles are opposites of each other, so they destroy one another. However, this process doesn't work exactly because some matter doesn't join up with anti-matter, leaving it left over.

These "leftovers" start to link up with each other to form protons and also neutrons. These are the building blocks of atoms but the universe is still so explosively hot that atoms couldn't form yet.

It took about 380,000 years before the universe had cooled down enough so that atoms could form. By that time, the universe was an enormous cloud of violent gases made of hydrogen and helium.

After about 300 million years, stars formed. They evolved from dense clouds of gas pulled together by gravity.

Gravity pulled together huge clusters of stars and they formed galaxies. The formation of galaxies would have taken place at the 500-million-year point in time.

Today, our universe is filled with planets, stars, and galaxies. It's continuing to expand.

FASCINATING FACTS ABOUT THE UNIVERSE

As the universe continues to expand, all the galaxies are moving farther and farther away from each other.

Albert Einstein thought there were three possibilities for the shape of the universe. It could be closed or it could be open, or the third possibility is that it could be flat. Most astronomers today believe that it's flat.

There are actually large empty spaces with no galaxies or other ordinary matter within the universe. These spaces are called voids.

The element that appears the most often in the universe is hydrogen and helium is second.

Astronomers believe that the universe is getting colder. It may freeze someday.

The universe doesn't really have a center. We've gone from thinking the Earth was at its center, then the Sun, then our Solar System, and then our galaxy. Since the galaxies are all expanding away from each other there is no central location. The universe doesn't have a fixed edge.

Awesome! Now you know more about the size of and lots of other facts about the universe. You can find more Astronomy books from Baby Professor by searching the website of your favorite book retailer.

Lightning Source UK Ltd.
Milton Keynes UK
UKHW050733021221
394882UK00005B/85

9 781541 913561